Winning the Customer

Understanding the mind of the customer

By: Cary Cavitt – M.A.
Author, Speaker, and Founder of
Service Starts With a Smile Seminars™

www.carycavitt.com

Copyright © 2017 by Cary Cavitt

All Rights Reserved

Other Authored Books

Service Starts With a Smile

Customer Service Superstars

Five-Star Service

Luxury Service

People Skills

The Enjoyable Golf Club Experience

Being the Leader People Want to Follow

Books may be purchased at:
www.carycavitt.com

Customer: \'kəs-tə-mər\

A person who decides whether or not to keep our doors open.

"One thing that really sets Cary apart from many other people is that he always seems to take that little extra time to say hello even though you know he is crazy busy. He stills can make you feel important."

Mr. Tom Lange
General Manager
Morton's the Steakhouse

◆

"Cary's light hearted approach coupled with his experienced professionalism cannot be beat.... Mr. Cavitt is someone I recommend in your corner."

Mr. Scott Van Jacobs
President
The Ark Candle Co.

◆

"Cary is truly a person of the highest integrity and has a genuine concern for people. I encourage you to take advantage of his expertise. You will be challenged and inspired to grow personally and professionally."

Mr. Rusty Trubey
Director - *Chi Alpha Christian Fellowship*
West Virginia University

"Cary is very witty and much smarter than he leads people to believe…He is successful due to his genuine love for people and interest in what he does. He totally believes he was put here on earth to enrich the lives of people he comes in contact. He has enriched my life and can do the same for you."

Mr. Bill White, PMP
Program Manager
Motorola, Inc.

♦

"I have known Cary for about 15 years and have seen many of the same people return again and again. Customer service is obviously #1 with him."

Mr. Rick Thielsen
LIGHTspeed Technology

♦

"Cary displays a unique commitment to people by his focus on personal service and satisfaction."

Mr. Todd A. Rowden
Attorney-at-Law
Riffner - Barber - Rowden LLC
President, Palatine Rotary Club

Table of Contents

Introduction......................

The Mind of the Customer...

Chapter 1
Makes a decision within 30 seconds...

Chapter 2
Is in a vulnerable position.........

Chapter 3
Would like to be acknowledged.........

Chapter 4
Would like a sense of belonging ....

Chapter 5
Measures how friendly we are.........

Chapter 6
Would like to be served.........

Chapter 7
Measures how willing we are to serve.....

Chapter 8
Would like to be treated respectfully...

Chapter 9
Measures how much we care.........

Chapter 10
Would like help in making a decision...

Chapter 11
Measures how knowledgeable we are...

Chapter 12
Would like to be listened to.........

Chapter 13
Measures our manners.........

Chapter 14
Measures our efficiency.........

Chapter 15
Measures our consistency.........

Chapter 16
Would like to feel appreciated.........

Chapter 17
Would like to trust us.........

Chapter 18
Some closing thoughts..........

The mind of the customer foremost wants to know if we can be trusted.

Introduction

As I approach my fourth book on the subject of customer service, I cannot help but arrive at the conclusion that the ultimate goal in providing great service *is to win the customer*. If we are to create loyalty, it becomes essential that we understand the inner needs of the customer.

Coming up with the idea to write this book is a result of having served over 100,000 customers as well as playing the role of a customer. My focus is to show what happens in the mind of a customer as he or she makes contact with an organization.

The goal in sharing these thoughts is to offer insights into how to exceed the expectations of the customer. My other goal is to explain the *seventeen essential needs* that must be met if we are to win their loyalty. By understanding these inner needs, we can then find ways to meet and exceed the customer's original expectations of our service.

Winning the customer will only happen when we consistently meet these seventeen needs. Every customer subconsciously is measuring our service based on whether or not we are meeting these needs. By understanding and then fulfilling these needs, we will eventually find more customers becoming loyal to our organization.

If I had to summarize the most important key in winning the customer, it would be to gain their confidence. Once obtained, we can be sure that the service we are providing is also meeting another important need…which is to trust us.

May your days be filled with providing excellent service to your customers!

Best regards,

Cary Cavitt
Author, Speaker, and Founder
Service That Attracts Seminars™
www.carycavitt.com

This book is dedicated to those who win customers simply because they can be trusted.

Chapter 1
The Mind of the Customer…

Will make a decision within 30 seconds…

The way to win customers in the first 30 seconds is to make them feel welcomed.

From the moment that a customer makes contact with an organization, a decision on the overall service will be made within the first 30 seconds. Whether we realize it or not, every customer will unconsciously measure our service. If we start off great, the odds are in our favor that we will win their confidence. But if the service starts off on the wrong foot, more than likely we will not see them coming back.

Because of the many available options in today's marketplace, the customer is offered a wide selection of similar companies to choose from. More than likely, the product or service that we provide is available in abundance. This is why it is critical to win our customers from the start. This first impression will go a long way in deciding whether or not we will be seeing them in the future.

The critical first few seconds is the most important timeframe for a new customer. They are in essence weighing whether or not they feel welcomed. If we give a great first impression, the customer will not only feel more secure in choosing us, but will also want to continue to do business in the future. If this first impression gives them the confidence that they made the right choice in coming to us, we will more than likely win them.

When a customer first enters a business, he or she is unsure about what kind of service they will receive. When we learn to graciously welcome them and provide a great first impression, it quickly dissolves any doubts and gives the customer the security he or she is looking for.

First impressions do matter. These first few seconds are critical in reassuring our customers that they have made a great choice in coming to us. How we perform during this initial introduction will stay with them for a long time.

The most important starting point is to offer each customer a friendly greeting and make them feel welcomed. Remember this tip and you will begin to win more customers to your side.

Chapter 2
The Mind of the Customer…

Is in a vulnerable position…

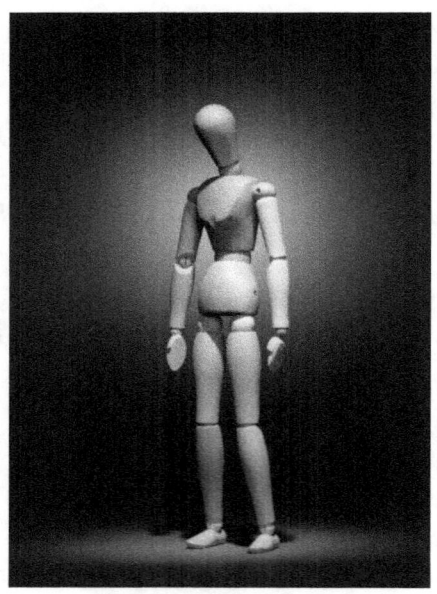

The way to win your customers is to show them that you enjoy being accommodating.

Customers are essentially in a position of seeking assistance in either purchasing a product or service, or are simply looking for information. Because of this arrangement, they are put in a vulnerable position. In other words, the customer is asking for help, and this in turns creates a subtle sense of insecurity.

Think of it in this way. Most people function from day to day without a need for assistance. But once they take on the role of a customer, they are now in a position of asking for help. This can create an inner sense of uncertainty due to the fact that they are seeking assistance.

With this being the case, it would only be reasonable that we attempt to win their confidence by being as helpful as possible. If we consistently show ourselves to be supportive and accommodating, we will quickly win them.

In a high percentage of customer service scenarios, the customer simply feels like he or she is intruding. They feel like an interruption. This is why many refuse to ask for further assistance. The customer has been given the impression that he or she is bothering the service representative and has learned to stop seeking assistance.

If we are to win our customers, we must never project an impression that we are too busy or do not want to be interrupted. We must show through our facial gestures and actions that we are happy to help them.

Customers will offer high ratings on the service provided because we have made them feel that we were approachable. We need to give them the impression that we enjoy helping them. Without this, we will never win customer loyalty.

One further thought is to remember that our customers will only feel at ease when we convey that we are there to happily serve them. When we express to each customer that we are accommodating, he or she in turn will be more comfortable and willing to do business with us in the future.

Chapter 3
The Mind of the Customer…

Would like to be acknowledged…

The way to win your customers is to acknowledge them with a friendly smile.

There is something powerful in acknowledging a customer through a friendly smile or a kind gesture. It expresses that we are available to help them with any assistance that they may require.

More importantly, offering a friendly sign of acknowledgement tells our customers that we have recognized them, and this in turn conveys a feeling of importance to them. What this also expresses is that we are happy and willing to lend a hand.

If we want to win customer loyalty, it is important to show that we are ready to help in a moment's notice. When we offer a friendly greeting, we are in essence telling customers that we are approachable and ready to assist.

But what happens when a proper greeting is missing? What does this convey to our customers? The first thought that comes to mind is that a lack of acknowledgement expresses an unwelcoming feeling to the customer. He or she has taken the time to make contact with our organization, and we have not properly recognized this.

When we do not show a friendly greeting, we are subconsciously telling them that we do not appreciate their business. It is as if we were saying that we really do not care that they have supported us.

The power of a warm welcome cannot be understated. It gives our customers a sense that we are happy to see them. It also tells them that we are user-friendly and available to assist at any time. More importantly, it expresses appreciation for choosing us.

Winning the customer is about treating them in an honorable manner. It is showing them that we care. Without an appropriate acknowledgement, we are telling our customer that he or she is not important.

Remember that a simple greeting will suffice. As mentioned, it can be a friendly smile or gesture that will do the trick. Show a warm welcome and watch what happens.

Chapter 4
The Mind of the Customer…

Would like a sense of belonging…

The way to win your customers is to create a sense of belonging.

When a customer enters through our door, he or she is measuring whether or not they feel accepted. This feeling of belonging will be a deciding factor in whether or not the customer will return in the future.

With this said, it only stands to reason that we should create an atmosphere where our customers feel welcomed and accepted. When we show ourselves to be friendly and hospitable, it gives them the impression that they belong. It also gives a certain sense of security by being warmly received.

The feeling of belonging is a powerful attraction because of the measure of security that it brings to a person. We all like the feeling of being somewhere that gladly makes us feel welcomed.

In the art of serving others, we must never forget that every customer has a desire to belong. Without fulfilling this inner need, our chances of winning them will be close to zero. We may provide great service, but without giving the customer a sense of belonging, we will only be spinning our wheels.

The best way to create a sense of belonging is by becoming skillful in greeting people. As mentioned in the previous chapter, a friendly welcome does not have to be elaborate or complex. It is simply showing ourselves to be pleasant and approachable.

Winning customer loyalty is about having the customer *want to return*. When we clearly understand this, we will begin to create a welcoming atmosphere that makes our customers feel accepted. We will also go out of our way in order to make sure that their needs are being taken care of.

In the end, *great service is about creating an atmosphere that attracts customers*. It is about creating a feeling inside that gives them the desire to tell others about their excellent experience. Give them this sense of belonging and you will win them back.

Chapter 5
The Mind of the Customer…

Measures how friendly we are…

The way to win your customers is to be friendly.

If we are to win our customers, it is essential that we are consistently showing ourselves to be friendly. Without this, we will never arrive at first base. Everyone is attracted to those who are genuinely cordial.

We will always be ahead of our competition when we have what I like to refer to as *the friendly factor*. It draws people in and quickly dissolves any earlier defenses. Friendliness has a way of making others trust us because of the way we have treated them.

To win the customer, we need to do things that show that we are amiable. This could include learning to smile more often. A simple smile is the surest way to offset any apprehensions that our customers may have when they first make contact with us. It quickly conveys that we are approachable and have a disposition that is good-natured.

Another great way to show our customers that we are friendly is to express an interest in them. By taking an active interest in others, we are conveying that we care. It may be as simple as asking an appropriate question that then allows us to learn more about them. When we show that we are genuinely interested, it conveys a friendly attitude.

Winning customers can never happen if we have not learned the friendly factor formula. Loyalty will occur when we learn to build sociable relationships. It begins with showing a friendly disposition and being genuinely interested in others.

When all is said and done, our customers will judge our service by how friendly we were to them. They will measure this based on how we have made them feel. If we are to win them back, we must consistently show ourselves to be pleasant.

Building relationships always begins by the simple act of friendliness. The proverb that states *"a man who has friends must show himself to be friendly"* holds true even in customer relationships. If we are to have loyal customers, we must show ourselves to be friendly as well.

Chapter 6
The Mind of the Customer…

Would like to be served…

The way to win your customers is to remember that they came to be served.

In order to win our customers, we must never forget that they would like to be served. It may sound elementary, but this simple fact is often forgotten in the customer service world. Customers enter with the desire to be taken care of.

One of the allurements of taking on the role of a customer is the anticipation of being pampered. Of course in reality this seldom happens. But every so often we are offered excellent service and look forward to the next time we have the fortunate experience of being served by what I like to refer to as a *customer service superstar*.

Customers enter with the hope of being served well. They secretly hope that our service to them will be first-rate. In their mind they desire to be taken care of that exceeds their original expectation.

But of course this rarely occurs. For many in the customer service field, their mindset is to take care of the customer in the easiest way possible. Instead of giving the customer an exceptional experience, many service representatives simply do minimal service without attempting to go the extra mile for the customer.

It is because of these continual experiences that most customers do not anticipate that the service will be anything more than average. But deep inside they desire that we offer exceptional service.

If we want to win our customers, we need to break out of just trying to get by with the service that we are providing and work toward giving our customers a great experience. We will create more loyalty because of the effort that is being put forth.

We must remember that customers first and foremost enter our door to be served. They anticipate average service, but secretly desire to be served in a way that makes them feel like VIP's for a moment. If we can do this consistently, we will soon find ourselves winning more customers who will tell others about the royal treatment that they had received from us.

Chapter 7
The Mind of the Customer…

Measures how willing we are to serve…

The way to win your customers is to be cheerfully willing to serve.

The superstars of customer service are noticed by their willingness to serve others. It is as if they feel honored to assist the customer. This trait alone is a major key in building a loyal following.

The mind of the customer is not only measuring the service provided, but he or she is also weighing our attitude and willingness to serve. They are unconsciously gauging our enthusiasm to want to help. Our attitude in performing the service will ultimately become the determining factor in how others perceive our service.

Consider the moments that you have been assisted by someone who appeared to be reluctant to serve. How did that make you feel? Did you walk away sensing that the service was average or below average? More than likely what you had recognized was an unenthusiastic attitude that made the service less appealing.

Now think of the times that you had received the best service. More than likely you encountered a service superstar who appeared to enjoy the act of assisting you. Their attitude made the service stand out. The reason for this is that customers ultimately measure the service by our attitude and willingness to serve.

Being willing to help others is essential if we are to win the customer. In my second book entitled *Customer Service Superstars*, I focused on the principal attitudes that make service superstars. In the end, the attitude that we have will be the determining factor in how our customers perceive our service.

If our attitude is right, we will show it in the way we serve. Instead of viewing our duties as simply following a job description, we begin to see our responsibilities as an honor to help another person out. Not only will this perspective make our service stand out, but it will also draw customers back again.

Remember that our willingness to serve is just as important as the service being provided. Customers expect to get service but will be pleasantly surprised when we do it with a cheerful attitude.

Chapter 8
The Mind of the Customer…

Would like to be treated respectfully…

The way to win your customers is to show proper respect.

If we are to win our customers, it is essential that we show proper respect. This is because conveying respect will consistently project that we appreciate their business. It also shows that we value them.

Without appropriate regard for others, it becomes difficult to create great customer service. Every person is attracted to those who show respect. This is one of the major reasons that respectful service representatives typically stand out above the crowd.

When all is said and done, our service will be measured by *the perception that the customer takes from the experience*. If he or she has not felt respected during their contact with us, they will more than likely rate our service as below average.

On the other hand, when we consistently show a respectful attitude, our customers will perceive the service as above average. This is the power of respect. *It enhances the perception that the customer has of the service being provided.*

As mentioned earlier, showing respect expresses that we value others. If we are to win our customers, it is vital that we convey this *sense of significance* to them. When we offer the VIP treatment, we are in essence showing respect.

We should always view our customers as important *simply because they are important.* Besides the fact that they are ultimately the ones who will decide whether our doors will stay open, our customers are fellow human beings. This fact alone becomes reason enough to honor them with respect.

Winning the customer has everything to do with making them feel worthwhile in having done business with us. It is having them walk away feeling that they were treated well and shown respect. When these two combinations are present, the goal of creating customer loyalty becomes more obtainable. Not only will they desire to return in the near future, but will not hesitate to tell others about us.

Chapter 9
The Mind of the Customer…

Measures how much we care…

*The way to win your customers is to have
their best interest in mind.*

Customers can quickly read how much we care by sensing if we have their best interest in mind. Without this, they will eventually look for another place to do business with.

Caring is a sure way to win customer loyalty. This is because everyone is attracted to those who genuinely care. This attitude also builds trust and loyalty because our customers sense that we are looking out for them.

Is there a way to develop this quality that will make our customers notice something different in us? What is the key in becoming a more caring person? These questions can be answered in two words: *really care!*

When we truly want the best for others, our whole outlook on life begins to change for the better. We start to treat others differently and become more thoughtful toward each customer. Without saying a word, our actions will show that we have their best interest in mind. Our customers will quickly pick up that we genuinely care that they are treated well.

So what does caring look like in the world of customer service? For one thing, the act of caring is shown in the way we focus attention on others. We recognize that our responsibility is to meet the needs of others. Instead of being self-centered, our life now becomes others-centered.

Another way that we show concern is by going the extra mile in delivering excellent service. When our customers notice that we have gone out of our way in meeting their needs, they in turn will think more highly of our service. *It is the small things that will make all the difference in how the customer perceives our service.*

If we are to win our customers, it is vital that we convey that we are looking out for them. It is showing that we care about their experience. When we do this, they will have a legitimate reason to tell others about our excellent service.

Chapter 10
The Mind of the Customer…

Would like help in making a decision…

The way to win your customers is to assist them in making the right decision.

When we are serving customers, it is important to understand that they are anticipating our assistance. In many cases, the customer is undecided and is seeking our advice. We can help guide them simply by listening and asking the right questions.

If we are to win the customer, it is essential that we learn how to lead them in making the right decision without appearing as if we are trying to push a quick sale. This is because nobody enjoys feeling as if they were being pressured. The key is to make suggestions that we feel would fit their immediate need and allow them to make the final decision.

There is a fine art in assisting a customer. We are to be there for them as well as be available to answer or offer suggestions. When we do this with professionalism, our customers will feel more confident in our suggestions. They will begin to trust that we are leading them in making the right choice.

A large percentage of customers who make contact with a business are unsure about making a purchase. They may be undecided in whether or not to buy a product or service. In reality, many are looking for a knowledgeable person who will lead them with ideas and additional information.

The important point is to remember that we are to gather as much information from them in order to offer suggestions. As mentioned earlier, we are there to assist without appearing like salespeople simply trying to make a sale. When we ask the right questions and then allow the customer to make the choice, it then creates a certain amount of trust in the relationship.

Our customers will not only appreciate that we took the time to listen, but they will also be won over by our professionalism. They will feel that we cared about their needs by the questions that were asked. They will also walk away with the feeling that we were very helpful. Find out what the needs of the customer are and simply direct them with the available choices that you offer.

Chapter 11
The Mind of the Customer…

Measures how knowledgeable we are…

The way to win your customers is to be knowledgeable in the product being sold.

Customers expect us to be experts in the product or services that we provide. They enter with the expectation that we are knowledgeable and can direct them in making the right decision. In essence, they are putting their trust in the information that we provide for them.

If we are to win our customers, it is vital to be educated in what we are offering. By being well-informed, we are giving them both the confidence and assurance that they will be directed in making the best available choice.

When a customer makes contact with us, he or she is in effect asking for assistance. They want us to be the experts in the product or services that are being offered. If the customer senses that we do not have sufficient knowledge, they will more than likely find another place to do business with.

We must remember that every customer is seeking something in their shopping experience. In the majority of cases, this seeking is simply looking for answers. They ask questions in an attempt to not only find information about the product or service, but also to test our knowledge. If we pass the test, the customer will then begin to put more confidence in the advice that we offer.

Winning the customer is about gaining their confidence. It is about having them trust the information that we are providing. Without having a high degree of knowledge, we can be sure that winning the customer will take place less frequently. It is only when we show a high level of knowledge and offer sound guidance that ultimately will win the loyalty of our customers.

Reflect back on the times when you were playing the role of a customer and had inquired about a certain product. Looking back, it was those who showed a high degree of knowledge who eventually won your confidence. In the same way, our customers will gain more trust when we show ourselves to have a high level of knowledge in the product or service being offered.

Chapter 12
The Mind of the Customer…

Would like to be listened to…

The way to win your customers is to listen and then ask the right questions.

Another sure way to win customers is by showing them that we are great listeners. Not only will they appreciate the fact that we have given them our full attention, but they will also feel that we genuinely cared about meeting their immediate needs.

Listening is a powerful communication tool. It conveys our interest in others and makes them appreciate that we have taken the time to clearly hear what they are saying. This is especially true with our customers. It expresses that we are there for them and attentive to their needs.

When the customer makes contact, he or she is in pursuit of information. They come with the goal of being provided with the best options available. By clearly listening to what their needs are, we are then in a better position to meet these needs.

Every customer would like to be listened to. He or she wants to feel that we have taken the time to really hear what they are inquiring about. One way to do this is to ask questions. When we listen and then ask a question back to the customer, it expresses that we are truly interested in what they have to say. It also tells them that we have heard them.

If we are to win the customer, it is essential to understand what makes them want to return. One way to draw them back is to learn to listen more. As mentioned earlier, learning to pay attention and ask questions is a powerful tool to convey that we are good listeners.

Instead of telling customers what they need, it is better if we ask open ended questions that will allow them to draw up their own conclusions. *Open ended questions usually start with Who, What, When, Where, and How.* These types of questions will give the customer an opportunity to fully explain his or her needs.

One final point is that listening also conveys that we are patient. When our customers sense this, they will appreciate the fact that we were more interested in their needs as opposed to simply trying to make a sale.

Chapter 13
The Mind of the Customer…

Measures our manners…

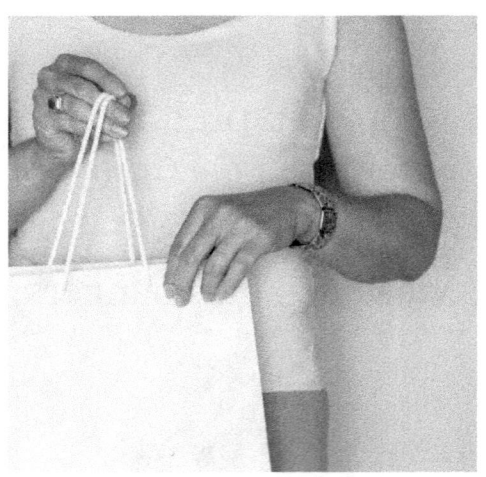

The way to win your customers is to show proper manners.

Great customer service is learning to exceed expectations. It is going above and beyond what the customer anticipated. To take the extra step and offer something unexpected will always give them the perception that our service was excellent.

One way to do this is to always offer what I like to call *good old-fashioned manners*. Being a person who shows himself or herself to have pleasant manners wins every time. Even though it may be seldom noticed in the world of customer service does not mean that good manners have gone out of style.

The mind of the customer warmly welcomes us when we show ourselves to be polite. Everyone appreciates when another person is thoughtful toward them. Not only does it attract, but it also creates loyalty.

When we talk about being a person of manners, we are mainly referring to our day to day conduct. In a sense, it is showing consideration and thoughtfulness. Simple phrases like *please* and *thank-you* reflect pleasant manners. Having the quality traits that display appropriate virtues can also express manners.

Whenever we are looking out for the best interest in others, we are displaying good old-fashioned manners. Our customers will respond positively and be won over by the proper conduct that we have shown.

Because genuine courtesy is seldom experienced in the marketplace, it is always refreshing for customers to be treated in such a way. Even though they may not say anything, we can be sure that our polite manners will eventually draw them back.

By going the extra mile and showing consideration, we are telling our customers that we not only value them as a person, but we also appreciate that they have conducted business with us. And in the end, we will discover that these good old-fashioned manners really never go out of fashion.

Chapter 14
The Mind of the Customer…

Measures our efficiency…

The way to win your customers is to respect their time.

One area in our service that will consistently be measured is our efficiency in providing excellent service in a timely fashion. Our customers will recognize when we have respected their time and will rate our service higher simply because of this.

Because we live in a fast-paced society, our customers would like to see that we serve them in a timely manner. Our goal is to show by our actions that we respect their time by being as professional and efficient as possible in our service to them.

When they take notice that we are serving in a way that conveys to them that we respect their time, they cannot help but recognize our service as being excellent. This is because we are conveying to them that we recognize that their time is valued.

Winning the customer is about making the transaction as efficient as possible. In the mind of the customer, he or she is measuring how much we are respecting their personal time. If they perceive that we are taking our time, the message being conveyed is that we don't really care.

In order to serve in an efficient manner, we need to fully understand the product or service that we are providing. We also must understand how to conduct the transaction as quickly as possible. When we understand the total process involved in serving the customer, we will begin to offer better overall service.

Nothing can be more frustrating for a customer than to have to wait for a transaction that should have taken half the time. When this occurs, the mind of the customer makes a mental note never to return again. In most cases, they will show their displeasure by simply not returning.

Being efficient gives our customers the impression that we are professionals in our field of work. It tells them that we value their time and want to make their visit as pleasant as possible. Offer this and you will consistently win the customer.

Chapter 15
The Mind of the Customer…

Measures our consistency…

The way to win your customers is to show the same consistency every time.

Every customer would like to know that our service will be consistent each time. They want to know that the great service they receive is going to be the same the next time they are doing business with us.

Consistency has a way of bringing security to our customers. Because our service maintains uniformity, it gives them the confidence that they will receive the same service in the future. When this happens, we can be sure that customers will want to return.

When our service is lacking in steadiness and stability, the customer then begins to view our business as unreliable. They feel that our service lacks any sense of direction and cannot be dependable. The result of this unpredictability is that the customer ends up looking elsewhere in an attempt to find more predictable service.

The importance of dependable service cannot be understated. This is why a consistent and friendly attitude is so critical in the world of customer service. When we show ourselves to be reliable and steady, we give our customers the security that they are looking for.

The mind of the customer wants to know that they will be treated exactly the same way each visit. They also want to know that the product is going to be the same every time. When this occurs, not only will they want to return, but they will also feel secure enough to tell others about the great service that they have always received from us.

Loyalty takes place when customers have the inner security and confidence that we will not change. They do not like change, especially when the service offered previously was outstanding. In order to do this, we must make sure that everyone on our team is on the same page when it comes to service.

When our service maintains this consistent pattern year after year, our customers will eventually come to expect that we will take care of them in the same excellent manner.

Chapter 16
The Mind of the Customer…

Would like to be appreciated…

*The way to win your customers is to show
that you appreciate their business.*

One of the best gifts that we can offer our customers is to convey to them our sincere appreciation for doing business with us. This will make all the difference in whether or not we succeed with them. Not only will it attract more customers back, but it also satisfies the inner desire to be appreciated.

When a customer does business with us, he or she has made the conscious decision to choose us over the competition. When we see it from this perspective, we in turn will begin to naturally show appreciation more often. This mindset of recognizing that every customer has other choices should make us all the more willing to show appreciation that they chose us.

Showing appreciation is a very powerful attitude. When it comes from a sincere heart, it attracts customers and gives them a reason to come back. We are in essence recognizing their true worth. This makes the customer feel valued to have done business with us.

On the other hand, if we forget to show the customer that we appreciate their support, we are expressing that we do not recognize their value to our organization. They walk away with an inner feeling that we do not recognize their worth.

Showing appreciation has a way of meeting the customer's internal desire for feeling valued. They will appreciate the fact that we have recognized their worth and give our service higher ratings. This simple expression of gratefulness will not only win customers back, but it lets them know that we recognize their importance to the success of our organization.

In order to show gratitude, it is important that we express it from the heart. Our customers will be able to sense when we sincerely appreciate their business. They will be able to tell when we genuinely are thankful for their support. This will also give our customers a reason to return in the future and tell others about the service that we provide.

Chapter 17
The Mind of the Customer…

Would like to trust us…

The way to win your customers is to be a trustworthy person.

The ultimate goal in providing customer service is to build trust in our relationships with those we serve. *This is because winning a customer will never happen if trust has not been established.*

From the start, the mind of the customer wants to discover if we can be trusted. Their most important quest is to find out if they can put their confidence in our organization. This will eventually be the deciding factor in whether or not loyalty occurs.

If we are to win our customers, it is paramount that we understand how to establish trust from the beginning. As mentioned, the customer is seeking clues that will signify our trustworthiness. He or she may be measuring the way that we show respect and consideration. It may be in the way that we communicate either through our words or behavior.

When we show ourselves to be friendly and willing to help, our customers are more likely to trust us. It really comes down to the little things that convey that we can be trusted. By showing ourselves to be considerate and ready to lend a hand, we will quickly express that we are reliable in providing dependable service.

To be trusted has many advantages when it comes to serving others. The biggest benefit is that our customers will not hesitate to tell others about us. They will gladly advertise our great service because of the trust that we have established with them. The confidence that they have in our ability will give them the assurance to tell their friends about us.

Without having credibility, the customer will more than likely find another organization to do business with. This is why it is imperative to establish trust from the start. The first impressions that are made will be difficult to erase if we do not show our best from the onset.

Winning the customer is really about winning their trust. It is about understanding their inner needs and doing our best to meet them. Be trustworthy and they will return.

Chapter 18
Some final thoughts…

*The way to win your customers is to enjoy
the experience of serving.*

As we come to a close, I hope by now that each reader recognizes that winning the customer is simply about *not forgetting the small stuff* that can easily be forgotten from time to time. Our customers are not asking for much except to be treated in a respectful manner. When we understand their inner needs, we will soon see more customers coming through our door.

Let's take another look into the mind of the customer and review the seventeen needs that must be met if we are to win them:

#1
The mind of the customer makes a decision within 30 seconds. *You can win them by being welcoming.*

#2
The mind of the customer is in a vulnerable position. *You can win them by being accommodating.*

#3

The mind of the customer would like to be acknowledged. *You can win them by showing a friendly acknowledgement*

#4

The mind of the customer would like a sense of belonging. *You can win them by being accepting.*

#5

The mind of the customer measures how friendly we are. *You can win them by showing kindheartedness.*

#6

The mind of the customer would like to be served. *You can win them by remembering that they came to be served.*

#7

The mind of the customer measures how willing we are to serve. *You can win them by cheerfully being willing to serve.*

#8

The mind of the customer would like to be treated respectfully. *You can win them by showing proper respect.*

#9
The mind of the customer measures how much we care. *You can win them by having their best interest in mind.*

#10
The mind of the customer would like help in making a decision. *You can win them by assisting in making the right decision.*

#11
The mind of the customer measures how knowledgeable we are. *You can win them by being well-informed of the product or service being offered.*

#12
The mind of the customer would like to be listened to. *You can win them by listening and then asking questions.*

#13
The mind of the customer measures our manners. *You can win them by showing proper manners.*

#14

The mind of the customer measures our efficiency. *You can win them by respecting their time.*

#15

The mind of the customer measures our consistency. *You can win them by offering the same consistent service every time.*

#16

The mind of the customer would like to be appreciated. *You can win them by showing that you are thankful for their business.*

#17

The mind of the customer would like to trust us. *You can win them by being a trustworthy person.*

In order to win the customer, we will need to fulfill these needs. By acquiring a better understanding of these unconscious requirements, *we will now be in a better position to meet and exceed the seventeen inner needs of the customer.*

Exceeding expectations of a customer is not difficult if we recognize that most expectations are actually quite low. As mentioned in an earlier chapter, most service performed on a daily basis tends to be average. This is because the majority of the seventeen needs discussed are never met.

I sincerely hope that each reader will begin to see that performing excellent service is really quite simple. Find out what the customer's inner needs are and fulfill them. My hope is that you will begin to recognize that providing excellent service is nothing more than giving our customers a pleasant experience.

If I had to close with a final definition of how to win the customer, it would simply be this:

"Winning the customer is nothing more than being joyfully willing to serve in a way that communicates friendliness, caring, and trust."

May we begin to see that serving is a great opportunity and privilege in helping others along the way.

About the Author

Since 1975 Cary has personally served over 100,000 customers. During these years he has observed and learned what truly brings customers back. Cary's zeal to find out what customers want has been his driving passion in building a successful career as a Golf Professional.

After receiving a B.A. at the University of Michigan and an M.A. at Eastern Michigan University, Cary then went on to receive his PGA Membership and become an award-winning Head Professional at various clubs in the Midwest.

Cary's expertise is in the area of customer service. Having authored various books on the subject, Cary has an experienced understanding of how to win the customer and exceed his or her expectations.

Because of his vast experience in providing over 30 years of personal service to a wide variety of clients, Cary is well qualified to coach others in what customers are really looking for when they make contact with a business.

Outside of his enthusiasm for teaching others the real reasons why customers return, Cary enjoys time with his wife Carol and their three children, Sara, Nathan, and Hanna.

Service Starts With a Smile Seminars ™

Helping America Serve Better

We offer customer service seminars to fit your needs for understanding why customers return. The insightful workshops are for both management and employees and are intended to build five-star service within your organization.

We offer Keynote Speaking, and *Service Starts With a Smile Seminars*™ that are available for the organization that is looking to improve on customer service. The fun and interactive presentation will motivate each team member to *want to serve customers more effectively.* Along with addressing why customers return, we will also explore *why customers choose not to return.*

If you are looking for a life-changing seminar of insightful applications for your organization, the workshops may be exactly what you are looking for. The positive changes will be felt immediately! More information can be found at:

www.carycavitt.com

Cary's first book, *Service Starts With a Smile* can be purchased at carycavittconsulting.com. In it Cary shares sixty-nine reasons why customers return. The insightful tips are great for those who would like to build a stronger service team and keep customers coming back time and again.

In *Customer Service Superstars*, Cary looks at what he considers to be the six most important attitudes that will influence every aspect of our lives. By understanding and improving on these highly regarded traits, our service as well as our own personal life will begin to change for the better. Visit us at carycavitt.com for more information.

Five-Star Service focuses on what great service looks like and how to consistently do it. The book is broken down into sixteen questions pertaining to customer service. The answers are simple and to the point and are a great reference and reminder of what it takes to bring about five-star service to our customers.

www.ingramcontent.com/pod-product-compliance
Lightning Source LLC
Chambersburg PA
CBHW070103210526
45170CB00012B/726